The Grapes from the Baobab

Ibrahima Amadou Niang

Translated from the French
by Ariane Baer-Harper

AMALION
PUBLISHING

About the author

Ibrahima Amadou Niang is a Senegalese writer, poet and political scientist. Niang currently heads the Guinea country office of the Open Society Initiative for West Africa. Prior to this position, he worked for the International Institute for Democracy and Electoral Assistance (IDEA) in Ghana and the Gorée Institute in Senegal. He studied International Relations and Economics at the University of Reading, UK; and for an MSc in Governance at Université Cheikh Anta Diop in Dakar, Senegal, from where he also completed a PhD in Political Science.

About the translator

Ariane Baer-Harper is the Director of Global Engagement and French teacher at Allendale Columbia School in Rochester, NY, USA. She started her professional career in Dakar, Senegal in 1998, and it was there that she discovered her passion for languages and writing. She holds a BA in Modern Languages from Hobart and William Smith Colleges and an MSc in Education from SUNY Geneseo, USA. She is currently working on her first novel.

The Grapes from the Baobab

Ibrahima Amadou Niang

Translated from the French
by Ariane Baer-Harper

AMALION
PUBLISHING

Published by Amalion Publishing Copyright © 2017

Amalion Publishing
BP 5637 Dakar-Fann
Dakar CP 00004
Senegal

www.amalion.net

Copyright © Ibrahima Amadou Niang
Translation Copyright © Ariane Baer-Harper 2017
All poems except indicated first published in French in 2010 by Amalion
Publishing in *Les Raisins du Baobab*. Poems in the section Beyond the
Baobab first published in English in this collection, except "In Our
Glances" and "Amaselly" first published in French in *The Prague Revue* in
2013.

ISBN 978-2-35926-069-4 PB

ISBN 978-2-35926-070-0 EPUB

Cover image, a detail of *Yóbbu Séet* (2016) by Djibril Fall Diene. Used by
permission and courtesy of the artist.

Cover designed by Djibril Fall

All rights reserved. No part of this publication may be reproduced,
transmitted, or stored in a retrieval system, in any form or by any means,
without permission in writing from Amalion Publishing, nor be otherwise
circulated in any form of binding or cover than that in which it is published.

Contents

The Humanist Momentum

Beyond the Baobab

Introduction

In his collection of poetry, *The Grapes from the Baobab*, written over a fifteen-year period, Ibrahima Amadou Niang invites us to join him as he embarks on a five-part transformative journey of self-exploration for a new Africa. Having known Niang throughout these formative years made it especially interesting for me to translate his work as it provided me with knowledge of the context surrounding his voice. When I first met Niang, he was a young man questioning his place in the world, and as the questions changed, over the course of fifteen years, from "what is my place in the world?" to "what is my contribution to the world?", I witnessed the voice of his poems develop from spectator to *engagé*. With each poem, we are able to see Niang's perception of the vital role that space and time play in this evolution, as in the very first poem of his collection, Little Dakar; where he understands that for any progress to take place in any environment (space), one must first observe the finer details: "A gentle waft of morning compliments / Travels through satin-veiled windows", and that everything has its time: "As we obstinately wait for midnight".

In the first part of his journey, Dakaroises, we find Niang as a young poet who, in observing the society around him in his native country of Senegal, senses a dichotomy between openness and convention in a world rooted in tradition. He expresses this tension in the poem Fatigue where he speaks of a "subtle aching", unable to find a reason for this pain yet knowing that he must overcome it. He uses the word "passerby" frequently in these opening poems, as he finds himself a bystander in the environment he had always taken for granted. He is the passerby, and not a main participant, aware that he must first have cognizance for the space in which he resides if there is to be change. Niang draws on all senses in his observation; the odors in the air, the colorful sights, the gentleness of wind, the smoky tastes of

Senegalese cuisine, and the cries of the people as they celebrate their independence day.

In Africa's Earth, Niang shows us the important and unequivocal role that nature, with his invocation of the seas, spirits, and his ancestral lands, must play in an emerging renaissance. Waters baptize, tall majestic mountains rise above and call people to order, and winds help carry them through the new changes leaving these agents of change scattered throughout the continent. In the final poem in this section, The Son of Anta Faye, the young poet offers hope and promise. He "dreams as night falls" about answering his personal call. Niang's ability to use the natural world around him to reach the spiritual world is how he can best honor Africa; the source of all life.

In the part Sutura, Niang 'refuses to be a spectator', 'refuses to be quiet' in this manifesting new dawn. He begins to resolve the tension between tradition and modernity by reshaping his definition of what it is to love a country, a continent, and a people. Rejecting the hypocrisy around him, he brings what he feels are the best parts of his tradition into the future. We see this best in the poem Gis-Gis which, in his native language of Wolof, translates to 'see-see', 'perception', 'perspective'. In Gis-Gis, written in the first-person, the narrator is Africa, and she opens by commanding us to 'look at the sky!' She goes on to ask us to no longer look at her with 'closed eyes', but to see her in a new light and to help her plant roots beyond the depths. This underground growth refers to the tradition that Niang understands he cannot reject entirely, for these growing roots of the baobab tree will create strong branches that extend far out into the future; branches which in looking like roots, challenge the observer to question where the roots begin and end, whether tradition is a thing of the past or whether it can also be something of the future.

In The Humanist Momentum, with Niang's new perception and definition, he bridges us to the next step in his journey where he discovers a newfound love for his continent. The strong roots of the baobab having been planted, the tree can now give us fruit. But not the fruit one would expect from the baobab tree, but something else that is known to come from somewhere else, a fruit that comes from this cross-pollination with worlds and cultures. Having found the importance of a new view: tradition leading us into modernity, we have the most traditional tree of Africa nourishing us with new ideas, and teaching us that there is no 'us' and the 'other', but rather that the 'us' can create the 'other' with a shift in consciousness. Not only does Niang challenge us in his poetry to change our view of Africa, but in growing grapes from the baobab tree, he also challenges us to change our view of the Other and what they can offer to humanity as a whole.

In the final section, Beyond the Baobab, Niang enjoins us to leave behind a limited view of Africa and the West, to look beyond the baobab trees and their outreached branches and fruits, and to join him in a unifying momentum of new ideas. It is in these poems that there is no clear line between 'us' and the 'other', but rather a combined humanism where we all have the ability to love, hate, get sick, and overcome.

The title, *The Grapes from the Baobab*, is born from this transformative voyage. First, the acknowledgement that every beautiful creation must have the correct space and timeline in which to grow; second, the fertile earth provides the perfect environment for the baobab to flourish; third, the strong roots of tradition plant themselves firmly in the ground; fourth, the grapes growing on root-like branches outline not only the importance of extended new roots into the future but of how Africa's new-found momentum can challenge and embrace such an extension while at the same time nourish tradition with new ideas; and lastly, the love that can be born when realizing the common humanism we all share and how each section of this collection unifies one to the next.

– Ariane Baer-Harper

Dakaroises

Little Dakar

Little Dakar
A gentle waft of morning compliments,
Travels through satin-veiled windows,
And leaves traces of passersby,
Passengers squeezed into large sedans, discreet,
Oblivious to the irritated glances from the street.

Aromas change brothels into cafés,
Vices become virtues with the break of day,
It's the hour when masks paint faces red,
Ashamed, their sullen faces hide fallen passions.

Little Dakar.
Swelling *Sutura* breasts,
Stretches out a marked past,
Relishing in the shapes and colors captivating our sight,
As we obstinately wait for midnight.

Dibiterie

The smoky odors of grilled meat
Turn my tongue rustic
To succumb to the fibers
Shredded by my impatient teeth.

The parade of the black woman before me,
As she walks back and forth, plates smoking from her palms,
Trembling rear softening men's glances,
More delicate than the foamy overflows
Of their brimming glasses.

She knows how to make these men desire her
They, whose fingers have perfected the caress of prayer beads,
Under the pretext of going for a walk
Have come to sit in obscurity
With milky cataract-infested pupils,
Chanting verses to reject the familiar.

And once success is found,
They shuffle into a prepared room,
To satisfy natural needs,
In the ambiance of carved beasts,
With the rhythmic chopping of flesh punctuating the air.

Ponty

Ponty and its froth delight the youth,
Soldiers on leave who have deserted their posts,
Doing as they please to the dismay of their parents,
Drunk and indulgent, frozen on the ground.

Far from worries, they dance on the tips of their toes,
Putting pressure on their heels which buckle in barbaric
pleasure,
Pushed harder than the *thiakaaba* beaten by a stick,
They beat and beat bitterness with a suited violence.

From conventional love and happiness,
They live sensuous affection,
Closer to a fleeting paradise than
A promised land.

And I see passersby wave their fleshy tails,
More hideous than their soiled bodies,
In search of the bull's eye
That will relieve them from their jaded lives
And return their lost dignity.

Fatigue

I feel no pain,
Not in my head
Not in my stomach
Not in my heart
Not in my liver.

I made no effort,
No laps around the track
No wrestling match
No algebra class
No long voyage.

I feel no pain,
Feet that tremble
Heart that rumbles
Eyes that sleep
Cheeks that swell
I feel weak.

I can't sleep
I can't sit
I can't think
I can't love.

I must put an end to this subtle aching.

Ay

I chanted your name five times
Breathlessly into my palms.
With teary disfigured face.

My throat knotted from grief,
I thought of your dreamless life,
Lived in the great reality
Of common misfortunes.

Who could offer you a voice
Across which you could speak to the world
And ask it to redeem the injustices
That you did not deserve?

Who could reconnect
The broken ties of your heart
More gracefully than the break of dawn
More deeply than the sex of an angel?

Ay!
Misfortune is never alone
No less than four times,
Child of Baol,
Talibé of the one who prays on the sea,
I never saw you drop your arms in defeat.

The world is your oyster,
Condensed dreams which patiently wait,
You dare tease them,
With the goodness of a blessed man.

Thiat

Thiat!
Call me nephew no more,
You are not my aunt!
Evil tongue of a snake
That poisons my body with venom.

Say my name no more,
You are not welcome!
In my life or in the one of those I love
I curse you.

Thiat!
Everywhere in my house
I will plant cacti,
Eucalyptus and lemon trees
To break your *Thiat*.

I will spit in my hand every morning
And will wash my face with it seven times
So that your evil eye does not restrict me.

I will hide away to be happy
In this world where eyes are as powerful as words.
Where the eyes of those who love you the most
Can bury you faster than a storm.

The Ferryman

They are seated there,
Uncertain travelers
Their dreams blending into hallucinations
As they watch the navigator of their illusions.
They know nothing of him
Yet he knows their dreams
He looks elsewhere,
Another sun rises.

In lightning strikes
The ferryman dodges the headlights,
While the ship glides
On the Sangomar.
His courage calms his team,
While mothers
Cry in rage.

He is young and handsome
A seducing liar
Worse for the youth
Than all the evils of long ago.

The ferryman who charms our children
With a brotherly smile
Invites them with a lot of pride
To die.

Fourth of April

You didn't decorate me in front of troops
But my solid chest is packed with recognition!

I have neither cap nor uniform,
No boots or pistols
I only have the love of a patriot
And the strength of a mother's sacrifice.

I will never have my initials
On this national flag attached
To the heavy pole inclined against my shoulder!

But I will always have love,
Blood to feed this earth of
Senegal with its generous soul.

My heart jumps
With the cries of the fanfare
Roaring Ninka Nanka
Leaves me weeping.

First of May

I never refused the parade,
To share the pride of the union.

I never refused to place in your hands
My grievances in a notebook,
To speak and think like an employee,
And finally dream about marriage.

To start a family,
With two, three children,
A solid and stable family,
Dependable like a leitmotiv!

But I have nothing to offer, my brothers
Unless my dreaming mind,
My loving heart,
My charming tongue,
My resolute faith.

I don't have a medal,
Nor a savings account,
Nor money to overdraft,
Not a thirteenth month,
Not a second chance.

My feet don't know airports,
My hands have never signed letters,
My parents have never received a thing,
And you speak to me about the First of May!

Workers have their day off,
As if their grit don't suffice.
They walk and dance,
To celebrate and lay claims.
But who would think to speak
For people like me,
Who will think of our First of May?

Africa's Earth

Zambezi

The days stretch across the prime of your bed
Warrior river with majestic airs,
Your eternal bathers, with morning smiles,
Celebrate life in their ablutions.

As you run to your eternal meetings
Victoria awaits impatiently
As she makes herself beautiful.

Your caress, like a cascade,
Weakens the aggressive nature
Of a near-fatal sweetness,
Along paths already marked by your flow.

Emotions so powerful, a renaissance,
With each glance, a permanent imprint of love,
With each call, the invocation of the mystical
Spirit of Nyami Nyami.
In honor of a savored majestic Africa,
In honor of all our brothers and friends.

As you run to your eternal meetings
Diarra dreams about this new Africa mounting her saddle
And Sulaiman and Youssoupha grin proudly
Towards Ndèye who murmurs a prayer.

Your caress, like a cascade,
Weakens the aggressive nature
Of a near-fatal sweetness,
Along paths already marked by your flow.
How I long to jump into

Your baptismal waters,
At the feet of a united Africa,
Whose current springs eternally.

Bassari

Bassari!
Better than an image on a postcard, I saw you,
I have not come to get rich off your name,
I have not come to take part in your exoticism.

Oh, land of sacred mountains!
Iwol rises high, in the distance.
A great and large promise on the mountain
Where Bédiks escaped from the converted mullahs
And took refuge in its isolated hills.

Not even one strand can match the beauty,
Of your women with their pierced noses,
Shaped by a porcupine's quill,
And the drunken stupor of your mystical winds.

Not far, silk-cotton or bombax trees,
Ceiba pentandra of the family malvacea,
Continuously serve-up renewed discussions.
Your trees with their delicious fruits,
Your soul with its baroque style.

I am going to leave now,
To the very edge of this venture.
To the very tip of a bumpy road,
In order to unveil your confirmed wisdom.

Pakao

To Banding Fossar Souané

Refuse captivity!
Pinet Laprade never took Sédhiou's fort.
His canons did not make you run away,
You Bérété warrior Prince of Mali.

Say no to assimilation!
You drank the blessed water of Sunna Karantaba,
To cleanse your fear and enter into civilization,
Rooted into your history like a royal baobab.

You will remain a symbol for generations,
Through your endurance and determination.
You represent a strong, victorious Africa,
Bearing the markings of renaissance battles.

Oh Jilang Sarr, Jilang de Fante Sarr!
You made a pact with the Sandiniéry genie
And with each new challenge
He washes the affronts in your waters.

Travels

You know it!
I didn't go to Treichville.

Between two trips
I stopped in Abidjan
To shake Fatimata's hand.

To eat alloco
In a hut in Bassam.
To meet Rokia
In the intimacy of The Baron.

I found joie de vivre
Happy innocence
A simple smile
Unrelenting beauty.

I pass by again and again
Without leaving my mark
But there my heart found
A reassuring warmth.

How I love to leave with no one seeing me
To hide myself with no one sensing me
To speak with no one hearing me
To love with no one betraying me
To write with no one critiquing me
How I love to fly with no one catching me
To curse with no one berating me.

These travels open my eyes,
Keeps my somber outlook at bay,
Tears me apart from my core.
My fear deserts me.
As I cling to this colorful soil
I feel at home somewhere else!

Don't tell me in which God I must believe
With which eyes I must see.
Don't tell me a thing
That is universal.
I am proud to be different
And that you are as different as I.
At the hour of departure
I throw myself on the tarmac
Like a plane ready to soar
High above a city.

The Wind's Watercolors

Through the window,
A swath of reconciled clouds
Locked tenderly.
Together, we have discovered
A message from a superior force,
And our fingers intertwine.

A blank canvas against the clear sky,
Magnifying this kente Sunday.
The wind teases the earth
With its moist paintbrush.
We follow these movements
Until our heads spin.

To make her understand this waste?
To penetrate the misinterpreted view?
Beauty forces itself upon everything.
The strength of the scenery reaches our sheets!
A last embrace before our final goodbye
Our eyes glisten with tears.

No, don't tell me!
I won't be able to stand it!
Leave like a thief
When I am under water,
Leave while the rain dilutes
The purity of our colors,
For the wind carries you
To immortalize our love
In the coming time
On this beautiful coconut coast.

That Is What I Was Telling You!

That is what I was telling you,
Accra hasn't changed.
In these times of skinny cows,
Its beef is still strong and greasy.

In these times of serious illness,
The women are well-developed and fertile.
Their curves bubbling over like volcanoes,
Our eyes fill with heat.

I love to blow the ashes of your smile
Over the charcoal of your flesh
That I may kindle burning words
So that your embers may ease my pain!

To drink okro soup with banku,
Its spices tickling my nostrils,
Bringing sensations from my country,
Where happiness once smiled upon us.

To meet Ruby in her splendor
Her warmth always makes me happy,
I would love so much to be near you
So that we might share
Intense moments of pleasure.

To walk in this heat,
Large beads of sweat drip down my face,
My throat dry,
My nose runny,
Blood flows through my veins.

Aunt Nana has kept her Queen mother smile.
Her face radiates from happiness and love.
Her graceful movements reassure me
As I discover virtue in purity.

Here is what I was telling you,
Accra hasn't changed!
And I am proud to be the son
Of this vast and endless land.

The Season Past

Let me go before the day comes
To dilute the glistening ink on the other bank.
I no longer sleep, no longer know reasons to love
The flowers of my thoughts are wilted.

Let me relax the muscles of my heart.
The gentleness of sleep in your oiled beauty,
Gives pretenses of farewell at this hour
Where genies come and free their secret lovers.

Let me smell the cool milk drunk by the spirits,
Who after a lively night of intoxication
And sumptuous songs of distress,
Recite their mass at the base of the baobab.

Sadly, it was the season past,
In honor of that which we sowed
Our dead, our traditions, our fate and our violations,
Are now lost in the golden sediment on the river's edge.

It was the season of aethiopes, strong and dignified,
Of wild and ferocious lions, noble insignia personified.

It was the season past. Forgive me, comrade,
If I deny myself the glories from overseas,
I must go far away, closer to my lost brothers
To those who no longer know how to speak.

The Curves of the Barangay

The curves of the barangay under the spell of trade winds,
The beaded pearls of their smiles illuminate my abandoned hut.

In this breeze perfumed with colored desires,
Their collection of dreams sits on the foamy crashing waves,
The smell of rum in the air inflames your words.
My protuberance engorged in my créole hut
The curvature of your buttocks adds to the honey-sweet taste of
your breasts.

The color of coffee, the color of sunset,
Such graceful and unparalleled charm falls from you,
That at night, you may marvelously defy the sun?

In this breeze perfumed with colored desires,
My blood, black with reason, blends with primary colors,
Without which passion could not exist
In the absence of an age-old victory.

These charms under the trade winds,
Form beaded smiles across my once-abandoned lips.
My black blood allows itself to try
When in your eyes my heart is reborn.

I Defy You!

You, Griot
I defy you
From chanting the names of my ancestors
Their victories and their powers
Better than their bloodline could.

I defy you
Oh master of tongues
From carrying my pain
With more difficulty than my flesh.

Run and tell the world
That the mouth speaks for itself
Stronger than the cords
Which tie your language to mysticism.

My princely Jolof voice
Guides the sounds of my memory
Louder than your tam-tam drums.

I defy you
From chanting verses
Other than those you were taught,
From speaking without invitation.

I defy you.
I have no wish to replace you
I have tried to go elsewhere
To look for praises.

Wounds from wooden sticks continuously scar my skin.
Put away your tongue until you can use your voice
To pronounce words that breathe life
Into your glorious Africa.

The Son of Anta Faye

There, at the summit of my willowy thoughts,
I contemplate as night falls on Bayakh,
Like rain trickling down the back of a birthing goat!
I revisit the cellar of my childhood,
Underneath the rotten planks of its existence,
Hope cracks open my heart
And like a broken promise,
Shatters the glass that gave me
As much happiness as misfortune.

I hear the honest notes
Played on your mystical flute,
They wound the deformed weeds growing
Under men's torsos,
Your silhouette revives the night's windpipe
Filled with fresh hopes.

Who are you?
Maleine the hippopotamus
Who helped the Mali dynasty endure?
You, the enemy of the river,
And of its already fertile sediment?
Golden foam which glistens like a teardrop
Dew on a heart broken by cowardice.
Son of the Fouta where Man offers his heart
At day for sharing at night fall.
Your heart is full of promised love.

Who are you?
Subhuman with seeping grace,
Your pores open to beauty

Like the petals of an intoxicating flower.
A wrestler with muscles made for an arena
You defend yourself from the caxaabals
Carried by the bakks of honesty.

I saw you between Bélinabé and Thilogne,
Somewhere in Kaédi, you opened your soul
To sweet suffering.
Why can I not wash all this goodness
Over the riverbank of your science?

But I learned in your hut that life is a painful memory
And the harmony of your flute guides my flock.
I dream as the night falls
Like a vast pool of promise.

Sutura

To Exist

In order to exist
I don't need to speak upon waking.
In order to recall my good faith,
I don't need to share endless memories
Taunting time that is already spent
From constant recollection.

To speak to say nothing,
A gut filled with pain.
To speak to be misunderstood,
A sacrifice of a terrible ritual.

I refuse to be a spectator!
I refuse to be quiet!
In this mess,
Where hypocrisy is covered in modesty.

Just Simply

To live simply,
Without court or faction
Without jealousy nor envy
To lay a small boat across a calm river
With nothing but a small fishing net
And a book to get away.

All around, nature lulls,
A conclave of rises and kites whispers,
And under the ruffle of the mangrove trees
The boat glides toward the river mouth.

A manatee tries to swim
Oysters cling to salty roots
Inlets extend as far as the eye can see.

Watching the setting sun
We know that the missus and her children await
As if separated much too long
They meet us with a lingering embrace.

I want to live simply
To awaken like an amnesiac who
Has forgotten the suffering of bygone days.
Who tries to live simply.
Just simply.

Butterflies

Let your ideas fly away delicately
Like the wings of the monarch
Who frees himself from all constraint
And flits through the open air.

Fly high without dizziness,
Far away from your misconception
Without attachment to dogma,
A momentary escape.

Dare to be transparent in all circumstances
A great challenge for a generation,
Money attracts like gravity,
To navigate cautiously.

Don't entrust your freedom to man,
Seek new challenges.
Open yourself to the world like a butterfly,
Who serenely soars
Towards imagined places.

That Age!

It's an age
I will never forget.
More painful than fifteen droughts,
With no drops or coolness to moisten
The shade of the hanging date palms.

I have lived through adversity
In the depths of my flesh without weapon
Made to fight against an old army.

I have lived through hardship like a roof
Without cornerstone to support its weight
And I almost caved in, had it not been
For my heart of man.

They threatened me
With underground missiles for naught
Hiding behind the callowness of my years,
A newborn waiting for the call to march!

I Am not the Others

I am not other people
And they are not me!

I understood this quite early
When everything connected us.
I longed for a good conscience
Without seeming so.

Speaking like you know you should,
A hint of a purposeful laugh
Conventional speech
Inherited gestures.

I am not other people
And they are not me!

Do you remember the day
I called you Miwo?
Your blood boiled!
But I tell it as I feel it.

I love to see you as you are
Devoid of fear and hate
Far from jealousy
As does contempt that plagues
Those who have things to forget.

How can I renounce my faith in you?
Tell me how I can denounce
My quest for strong feelings?
My divinity-seeking self?

If I will not be the other
They will not be me.

Diplomas

Bring me some fire
So that I may fuel its flames
With the ink of my sweat,
My sentence of many years.

I gave up my childhood
To age before my years
In the country that regurgitated me!
The North welcomed me in its knowing temples.

What should I do with all these papers
When they serve as tickets to nowhere
A life of disorder
Deceitful diplomas
Who don't keep their promise.

When I return at night,
When my daughter asks me for tight jeans,
My throat tightens with bile!

Curse these diplomas!
They once made me a superhero
But, now, as if in a bad dream,
They take forever to wake me up.

I Dreamed

I dreamed Dem Nga Dem Nga, stone-faced child
Of the hands of the brave men who shook the sea
Of the smile of the children whose barely tamed hearts
Devoured life with immortal momentum.
I saw my body as a newborn in the arms of my mother
Warmed in her assuring touch.

I am weighted by this freedom,
An insolent nomad, an inspired poet,
Untouchable, crafting syllables and vowels.
Manipulating feelings with my pen to create paths
To connect idle hearts eager to discover
The grandeur of being before dying.

I sharpened the stone through the magic of my verbs
I said Dem Nga Dem Nga, stone-faced child
My father will renounce me
Of me he will not be proud.

Pork Sausages

Red lips, pink tongue
Pork sausages.
Here are the foolish things mothers
Teach their children.

In their imagined world
Faith is expressed through
Consumed foods.

In their imagined world
Faith is expressed through
Sipped drinks.

These believers who adore
Pork sausages
They must be wary of,
Their lips are red,
Their tongues pink.

But he's a Freemason,
I know what I say!

Ah! But he's gay,
I know what I say!

Him, over there, he's a thief.
I swear my life on it!

Tongues wagging between frustrated men,
Who can't look each other in the eye,
Who can't live their lives,

Frustrated of tied hands.

And when you remind them
That one of their own is involved
They shine in hate forever.

The Devil is other people!

Njoloor

I saw them bury a man,
While the earth was smoking hot

His assembled children take heavy steps towards the tomb,
Begging for time as they stare at his cadaver
What would they have forsaken to not live this moment
But they must entrust their father to their Creator.

Alone, in front of the hollow grave, the oldest digs in his foot,
Across from him, the youngest slides his right leg back and
forth,
Helped by those near, they carry the corpse under discreet
sheets,
And with skilled hands the body is angled.
He descends calmly into the tomb under holy invocations.
Pass them a knife so that they may cut the cords!

A moment of silence broken by shovels of dirt.

We get on our knees to pray for this man,
Because God alone knows how he lived.
His sons can only hope.

One last look, and everyone leaves with a heavy heart.

Njoloor!

Lunch barely eaten, all energies are lost
In this heat and misfortune that strikes our
Dear ones whom we had hoped to never see suffer.
Maybe it's an illusion that creates this enormous heat.

Maybe this is all a bad dream.
Maybe genies seek to warn us?

I say no!

Death comes often between the noon and the zenith of our lives
Where God turns off the light to guide our souls,
Like the spirits who kill the passersby at Njoloor.
Faith, comfort those you convene in eternity.

Legacy

What would you have become
If your father hadn't lived each day
As if each opportunity was a building site
As if it was his last?

What would you have become
If your father hadn't sacrificed himself
Living with just enough strength
To ensure the future of his children?

He left you with endless land
Replenished bank accounts
Well-built homes
Well thought out customs.

Yet you decided that you would suffer no more
Not even to preserve what he had left you
You squabbled with your brothers
And squandered it all away.

The ideal of family swept away
To the depths of desperation
Where, at the hour of sharing,
Brothers patiently wait with mortal jealousy

When the wives got involved
And remembered their dreams of dynasties
The spirits of the husbands lost their way,
And hastened the family to this desolate chasm.

Forgive us father, we were not worthy of your legacy
Which was above all the cement
That held us together.

Forgive us father,
We would have been better off inheriting your wisdom
Because fortune is easily passed down,
But the future must be built together,
The future is a brotherly momentum.

Gis-Gis

Look at the sky as the rain comes!
Its somber color announces the Renaissance.
And the image of a life unfolding,
Reflecting your soul and its radiance.

A fertile soil across the plains,
From which your seeds bloom into grains.
Already, you see me with eyes closed
To seek dwelling in the dawn of your supremacy!

I am Africa, a woman who breathes monsoons.
In my darkness you feign to see me,
Yet, I am neither a martyr nor doomed!
I have never raised armies to conquer land,
But to build an empire of humanism and honor.

I no longer wear the color of suffering,
But one that opposes iniquities and alienation of faith.
Oh, Land! You don my color to mourn your deceased,
Attracting compassion from those who speak peace.

I am the anchor that moors civilization,
A rising sun that invades your sleep.
In my soul you get drunk on science and love
Its vision offers you benefits to reap.

I exchanged a thousand golden jewels from Djenné
For the freedom of my sons,
A hundred lions led them
Out of exile to the land of glory.

Many sacrifices have espoused
Miracles to previously impious eyes!
I am the tomb of Mogho Naba
Prince of Tenkodogo.

Divinity with a man's gaze, a primitive freedom!
It directs a thousand bird flights
Across forgotten, lush lands.
My spirit plants roots
Beyond the depths.

Inch'Allah

Inch'Allah,
You can be exempted from reproach
Just by saying it.
This divine decree crowns you.
You must know it.

How many times did you say it to me,
This dependable promise?
I always believed you,
Helped by my great faith.

I want to tell you friend,
Don't transgress your Creator!
Rise and march,
Because it won't be done in your place.

Another Gorée

I know another Gorée
Far from where tourists weep
Their souls moved by the evocations
Of a painful past.

Far from the exotic ochre building
And flowers more beautiful than promises
That bestow a signature portrait to the Island.

Far from Coumba Castel
And tantalizing smells of grilled fish
From restaurants eager to gratify thirsty buds.

Far from the ferries
And the charming signares.
The watchful eye of Blaise Diagne
Overlooking the women selling *thiaaf*.

I know the Gorée of Knowledge
The one made up of lyrical souls who embrace each other
In front of new and life-saving ideas.

The Gorée of a new impetus,
Of a renaissance,
Of a leap forward
Of self-reliance.

When the desire hits me
To jump into its delicious water
I hold my breath, and advance across empty pages
Virgin sheets for me to corrupt.

The Humanist Momentum

How I Love You!

Give yourself up one last time
And die.
If we must,
We'll do it together.

How I love you!
To be hidden from no one,
I would love for you
To tell me secretly,
That you will always love me too!

Because my love for you
I carry,
Like blood that
Irrigates my veins
With a force.

Siga

My Gelawaar, your beauty strikes fear in me!
Your *petaaw* eyes challenge me early in the morning,
Your copper-toned skin embeds my heart in its cavity.
I am moved by your carnal smile,
A white grin of fine salt from the Sine.

If I could reside in the perimeter of your lips,
I would only come up for air when you cry.
Your tears would water my thoughts,
So dry from years of wandering.

If I could be a painting in your bedroom,
I would watch over you every night as you sleep.
Or I could be the pillow upon which you lay your head
To whisper soothing words into your ear.

Siga, your heart is more blessed than the water from the
Kaloum well,
And I won't be enthroned at Paaleen Dëdd
Just to become your Damel.
No!

Not even a spiritual bath!

I saw you at Buur Siin in Diakhao,
In this *djaneer*, our destinies intertwined.
I refuse to make libations under the Kanger Baobab!
To kneel before the tomb of Burr Siin Coumba Ndoffène Fa
Maak!
To dance and sing in order to lay claims on your love.
I will never make a pact with the gods.

Ah, my pagan soul!
I will drag it though Soror, Godaguène, Ndidor,
Tela, Maronem, Ngekor, Ndofene, and Ndielem Farha
Will conquer your body, heart and soul
With the sweet song of seduced men.

Ah, my princess, your smile leaves me shaking like a palm leaf,
And when your silhouette breaks through the shadows of the
gates,
My leaves will fly up, away from the brambles
To never again fall from the heights of death.

Saaxar

I only smoke when the ground is cool,
So that the purity of my words
May stain your amber-colored smile.

The wild sky asserts itself,
Its sealed vault goes bankrupt
At the dawn of boundless horizons,
At the eruption of out-of-tune prayers
Which come in the form of tormented thunder.

Look at this tree
The vegetation perfumes my gaze
Under the spell of nightly charms.
And I am only reflected by the gliding
Of your smoky body
Drifting towards deadwood hedges.

And I can only be moved by the unscrupulous touch
Of your *némali*-perfumed hips
And your clicking *jal-jali*
Like a pair of castanets.
What a delicious morsel!

Letter

I was never able to tell my father,
That I wanted to go to the beach,
Unless I asked him in a note,
Under the guise of his friendship.

To declare my love to a woman
Without writing down a thoughtful preface!
Placed in an envelope with a few leaves of lemongrass
And sheets of fragranced paper doused in my favorite scent.

To speak to a lover on the other end of the line
Without having first prepared a speech,
And the turn of events having been already identified,
A well-written poem in my hand would I preach.

Yet now I wish to mail you a letter, my friend,
A letter that no postofficer can deliver
That no messenger can send.
This message is too heavy to be carried.

I want to ask you to never leave me!
And I will write it in Indian ink
I will ask you to never betray me
I will mark it with the marrow of my bones.
I will implore you to never stop loving me!
And I will write it with holy water.
I will beg you to never die!
And I will sign it with my blood.

Rokiatou, never die!
Never die if you don't want my heart to collapse

Without me ripping it apart to offer to the wild beasts
Who would wait to satisfy their hunger with my unending
pain,
Ah, how I feel my veins snicker.

She mocks my loving blood as it turns in circles
Before it finds my trembling fragile heart
Which beats faster at the invocation of your name.
Miwo, my woman with the wild curves.

Yes, I will mail this letter,
I will mail it into the wind,
And in that way, at least the seasons will know.

High-Wire Act

Just like that, we allowed ourselves
A taste for yearning
By the innocent flight of vowels
Falling loosely from the mouth
Of the Beloved.

Should we think to arrange them,
Before hearts start to tremble?
Before reason takes hold?
Excessive zeal in
A proud passion which
Takes its time to take the reins.

Your resplendent voice turns me into a sirocco
Which lifts my immortal body
In a sacrificial soar.

I conquer you weighed down by levity!
Condemned to endure the sky's lightning.
Why am I forbidden to you,
When we are both equals?

I won't boast of my skin, my blood.
I will walk in circles, my blood.
To become a free lover
Who is only able to tempt through his words.

You Stole Her From Me, Ngoor

Ngoor Faye,
The night unfolds on the green riverbank of my youth
And eats away at the sand-castle of my emotions
Which used to warm me during the winters of my heart.

But where has my Khémesse gone?
She who is the adjective to my happiness?
She who is the adjective to my fleeting pain
Freeing the shadows of time.

I saw her leave towards Pokham,
Her veiled beauty, veiled my heart,
Whereas the heat of the Saloum drinks my tears,
The thirst in my heart cannot be satisfied
By this pain that leaves water spots on smiles,
Childhood silt cannot take the place
Of the clay which molds man,
But man must live in order to die a child,
Because childhood is a worthy life.

You stole her from me, Ngoor!
My Sérère with the heart of a shepherd,
Who led the flock of my thoughts through my youth,
When spirits confided in me with the secrets of the dead!

You stole her from me!
You, Okonkwo, this smile
A seed farmer of my culture
That I see, still perched
On the watchtower of my memories.

You stole her from me!
But she won't leave the refuge of my heart
Because I will only come out at the dawn of life.
But what is she, this convergence who harmonizes our hearts?

Election

Without system or ballots
I elected you as the supreme leader of my soul!
Without lies or promises
I gave you the keys to my city!

Sophie Sanou, you are the chosen one!
With sanctions, with pain,
No one needs to come and try
To corrupt my heart
Already affiliated to the party of your love
For which I will forever be partisan.

Winds From the Var

In the vineyards of Saint Laurent du Var,
The caress of the summer winds carry versatile
Bursts of jasmine on the back of its fragrance.

Red tomatoes and wild figs dominate the countryside
Cascading down the rolling hills.
In the middle of this world a sturdy lady sips
From a cup of tea, whose leaves were dried on another land.

In cool mountain breeze
She stops from time to time to tie her hair back in the wind,
And breathes the pure air which reminds her of day breaks
In a far-away country where she prophesizes.

On her left, a young black man she calls "my son",
"My daughter", as she addresses the one sitted to her right,
"You are truly my family".

Nomadic

Nomadic like water
In all its forms
It's everywhere
Nature has left a void.

Nomadic like wind
Across all the seas
Bringing cool air
To where it is most lacking.

Nomadic like soil,
Waiting patiently
Yet turning round and round
Opening itself to the world.

Nomadic like fire
Which brushes over hearts
In order to fan the flames
Of a peaceful light.

This Table!

They are all seated there
At least once a year.
While circumstances
Still allow for family to gather.

Without complexes or grudges,
We place a cake
Carefully chosen for the occasion.
Adding to the lovely black forest
Several fragrances will follow…
The small platter of spring rolls,
The decorative bottles of juice.

Around the table children run,
Friends chat in reunification.
This room is ready
For a grandiose moment.

It's done! The lamps are lowered
From the candles emerge a glow
Which magnifies these newly-captured days
With much love and tenderness.

We croon a well-known song
Astound at the men who know how to feel
For such a birthday
Around this very familiar table.

Ëlëk

Another day, to other hours
I dream like a shepherd,
Who swings his crook back and forth,
As if to rock the crazy thoughts
That latch worriedly to solitude.

I will no longer be part of those who don't know what to do
I will no longer be part of their lives emptied of courage and
hope.

I will no longer be part of those condemned to silence,
Out of fear that I may no longer live a few moments of glory.
I know that she is waiting for me
At the end of this road.

Beyond the Baobab

In Our Glances

These colors that you bring,
Keep my memory speechless.
This trouble that you go through
To instill me with hope?

On the hills of Ngozi,
In the copper tone of the harmattan,
Chasing after time ages us,
And all the while, you wait for me.

Under my hair I had kept from you
An innocent mind
Full of delicious clichés.
Full of ardent passion!
On lemongrass leaves,
I had harvested "I love yous"
Elongated and beautiful
As long as I sowed these seeds.

On the honey pot,
Our eyes drifted apart,
And you, who saw yourself already old,
Meditated on happier days.
The gray eagle of cruel fate
Without invitation took hold of our glances,
Plunged them to the earth below,
Now scattered, mapped out by the gods.

The Old Pelican

The last of the day's yellow rays
Stretch out and embrace nature
With thousands of voiceless birds decorating the landscape.

An old pelican floats atop the water
In the lagoon that has been its home for many moons
A lump stuck in its old throat
As it curses the day that it swallowed that old carp,
With steel scales grating its throat.

Abandoned, it swims against the current
Executing the dance of the dying.
The smell of the end is in the air,
Here, the terminus to the long journey
Of a great sailor who had defied the high seasons.

It is this final swim,
Imposed by the swift stream
Which will dispose,
Its aged body to die alone on the shores.

Amaselly

Yellow smoothness
Spread across your bed
White flesh
Temperate on your skin.

Your pores boil
Your breath warm
Your eyelashes flicker
Like thick cinders

The seductive lava
Of your delicious kisses
And your eyes discover
Relentless torture.

Amaselly,
The fragrance of your neck
Aspires envy,
And tumultuous fertility.

I Had Imagined You

Finally the day I had awaited
Having prayed that time would freeze
Slipped through my fingers
Before I could seize it.

I would have painted it in gold and blue
On old papyrus ablaze
With sap from the sugar gods
On the trails leading to your heaven

I had imagined you naked
Your delicious inexperienced tongue
Nursing me with sweet words
And feeding me lively wild hope.

I had imagined you great
Your hair soaked in lotus
Your majestic arms hanging
Down a body carved from cactus.

I had imagined you Nefertiti
Goddess of sacred beauty
Who would give me the desire
To love you for eternity .

But when I got there,
You had just gone away,
My wait had lasted too long,
And all that was left of hope
Was a trail of smoke.

Finally the day I had awaited
Praying that time would freeze
The flower of wilted dawn,
When another man took your hand.

It Didn't Take Much

It didn't take much of
A blink of an eyelash
A reptilian assault
For me to bid you farewell.

Had it not been for this recollection
Ignited by this unexpectedly beautiful song
I would have directed the ship's bow
Towards the vast unknown.

I would have swallowed oceans
Inhaled hurricanes
Devoured the harmattan winds
Just to kill time.

But I had forgotten,
That it was enough for me to love you
Without expecting a return,
Without claiming your love.

All These Moons

I have kept watch over all these climes
To catch a glimpse of stars that smile
Feeling the dried sweat
Off the bristled barks of trees.

I kept vigil on the day,
Wanting to be its elder
That would guide it along
The paths I had already carved.

Never arriving
Never giving up
Waiting at the gates
To mourn night's death

But it had been buried
Long before my arrival
Without my seeing it
Night's beautiful tomb of wood

When will I get to mourn
These forgotten days
As dusk creeps in
Before this unscrupulous day?

Stigma

The waltz of the damned,
Is the dance of our land.
The do re mi spins us around,
Burning our feet to the ground.

Do you prefer to hunt than to dance?
Ebola's rhythm will give you that chance.
Or perhaps you wish to be admired,
Like in a gala before the music has expired.

My smile is contagious,
Love and friendship courageous.
Yet, happiness can only be obtained,
When Ebola has been contained.

Extreme mistrust
Ignorance acute
Do not ask me thus,
If we travel the same route.
Because my answer will be plain –
Guinean and human,
Liberian and earthling,
Sierra Leonean and game,
We are not the same.

Grafting Sap

You my beautiful tree
That I had always assumed
Were made of marble
Your trunk firmly secured as you bloomed.

Your roots plunged into the diamond Earth,
Shaking the ground like thunder
Singing infectious rhythms of Bembeya
That traveled from Dalaba to Fria.

But as the bats invaded you, my tree,
Your trunk unearthed and spun,
As they devoured your fruits and progeny,
The wood started to rot from within.

In time, your graft grew
This transformation anew,
Her power dominated your view
As she carried you through.

Oh, my beautiful tree,
Who with your sap do
Feed the spirits of men,
It's time for us to rise!

Kiridi

My trumpet exclaimed!
The air silenced its echoes.
My tongue proclaimed!
Saliva silenced its echoes.

My foot it paraded!
The Earth silenced its echoes.
My whole being invaded!
Fire silenced its echoes.

And those in my heart,
Ebola has sent to the ground,
It breaks me apart.

Yet, I will not back down!
I look to the *kiridi*,
Wandering child of Siguiri,
Whose parents died embracing in Conakry,
Does it mean he will have the same destiny?

Rice fills me and eases my rage,
I want to grow, feed and cultivate
This I do know, the fruits of old age
That will not condemn but will decide a different fate.

Unclean Crimes

Committing sin
In times of disease,
Ultimate suffering
For those it does seize.

But we are not vermin
Infesting soiled bins,
Nor are we parasites
Invading your kin.

Though the scents
Of perfidious death,
Brand those it torments
As it steals their last breath.

As I vomit
My dark skin decays,
My eyes have no respite
My face hollows and grays.

As I'm so cold
As my weight thins,
Last moments unfold
My aches dependent on fate.

The sap of my blood
Irrigates the field no more,
It runs through me, the color of mud
My exhaustion never abates.

Oh brother, what have I done?
I am the shunned one.
My fear, like yours, paralyses me,
But mine has already dug my destiny.

Ebol'Art

Broth made of our wings
Emits promising perfumes,
Titillates my singing nostrils
Tickled by the odors of plumes.

Bright colors adorn words of hope
Across the wall they are painted,
Our dreams tie them together like rope
Yet, the ground becomes tainted.

Paintbrushes and pens
Design the canvas of life,
Exposing all the great men
Who have endured this great strife.

But what she stole from me –
A liberty which should have been free,
My acts will pay for what she took,
Hope now seen through the eyes of a crook

We cannot escape to places unknown,
Another fate has been sewn
Traces of paint now chipped and faded,
Reminiscent of promises that she had made.

Glossary

Ay: hassle or misfortune
Bakk: wrestlers' war dances
Baraka: luck (in Arabic)
Barangue: colonial style straw houses found on some islands
         near the Indian Ocean
Bolong: inlet sinks into the continent
Caxaabal: wrestling technique
Ceeli: eagle
Ceibapentandra: kapok tree
Damel: title given to the king in the Cayor kingdom
Djaneer: morning dream
Ëlëk: tomorrow
Gelawaar: dynasty of noble warriors who founded the first
         Sereer kingdoms in the 14th century
Gis-Gis: point of view
Inch'Allah: God willing… (Arabic expression)
Jal-jali: sound beaded belts worn by Senegalese women on their
         loins to charm their spouses.
Kac-kac: sound emitted by the beads worn by Senegalese
         women around their loins, erotic symbols (onomatopoeia)
Kiridi: orphelin en langue Soussou
Lëpaalëp/Leupaleup: butterflies
Missiles sol-sol: talismans (expression used by the Wolof)
Miwo: sweetheart (in Tagouana language, Ivory Coast)
Ndënd/Ndeund: little drum
Njoloor/Ndojoloor: when the sun is at zenith
Némali: aphrodisiac perfume
Nyami Nyami: Godess of the Zambezi river
Ninki Nanka: mythical snake or dragon with scales. Famous
         song of the Senegalese army band
Pétaaw: cowrie shell used by fortune tellers

Sakhaar/Saxaar: smoke
Sangomar: land advanced in the Atlantic ocean
Sopi: change
Soutoureu/Sutura: modesty
Sunugaal: Senegal
Tchim/Cim: onomatopoeia characterizing contempt
Thiaaf/Caaf: grilled peanuts
Thiakaaba/Cakaaba: Senegalese dancer on stilts
Thiat: Evil eye

About the Publisher

Since 2009 **Amalion Publishing** has established itself as a publisher of high quality and critically acclaimed non-fiction and literary works on Africa. As an independent academic publishing initiative based in Dakar, Senegal, we are driven by the mission to publish and disseminate innovative knowledge on Africa to strengthen the understanding of humanity. Our works strive to promote a broader understanding of Africa and its people by providing a platform for authors to express new, alternative and daring perspectives and views on people, places, events, and issues shaping our world.

Amalion Publishing targets a wider readership of scholars, academics, students, and other readers seeking to know more about their lives and societies through monographs, textbooks, journals and literary writing. It publishes primarily in English and in French, and is willing to consider initiatives and ideas to disseminate in Portuguese and other African languages with a potential for wider distribution.

www.amalion.net
www.twitter.com/amalion
www.facebook.com/AmalionPublishing

www.ingramcontent.com/pod-product-compliance
Lightning Source LLC
Chambersburg PA
CBHW031002090426
42737CB00008B/636